PROJECT MANAGEMENT GUIDE

Manage Projects Like A Pro

By

Meenakshi Narang

TABLE OF CONTENTS

Project Management Guide

INTRODUCTION

Thanks for downloading this book titled '*Project Management Guide: Manage Projects like a Pro*'.

This book includes real-life scenarios and suggestions for managing small-to-medium-to projects.

At present, the use of Project Management is very helpful. Be it in the management of any academic project or professional one, it is good to have enough knowledge and managerial skills so that one can stay ahead in the rat race.

A great deal of learning comes with Project Management that consequently goes on to build professional credibility. Getting a grip over skillful management of projects certainly increases the chance of being a good leader.

This book is relevant for its comprehensive information covering various facets of Project Management. Hope this book can help you in managing your projects effectively and get the end results with flying colors.

CHAPTER 1: PROJECTS MANAGEMENT AND ITS RELEVANCE

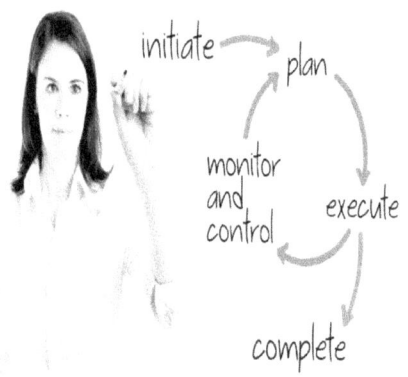

Project Management isn't actually new to many of us. This term is often used in higher studies or professional life. Let us delve deeper into the definition of this term so as to understand it in a better way. A very simple definition of "Project" is–

"A project is a series of well-planned tasks that you undertake keeping in mind various limitations such as time, resources, and the desired result, etc."

Thus, the word "project" leads to the connotation "before an action". Therefore, Project Management refers to –

"The process of implementing knowledge both functional and technical, skills and techniques in the day to day project activities to manage it effectively and efficiently."

TOWARDS A WINNING PROJECT

Management of project isn't always easy. It is imperative to know what makes a project successful. . A project must be supported with following features if you want to achieve your desired goal. - –

Create an Intelligent Idea – A plausible and a convincing idea is the pre-requisite of a successful project. Get a thoughtful validation of the idea lest it may die out at a later stage and cause a great deal of disappointment. The idea should be based on market research before it becomes the foundation of a project.

Think of Business Goal – Any project, however ambitious, is likely to go haywire if it is not backed up with a clear business goal. Having a categorical business goal will leave no room for confusions, making it easier to plan and manage strategically.

Set milestones – In the absence of practical and reasonable milestones, a project is likely to lose its steam and unlikely to meet the set deadlines. Setting up milestones would further help in making the project financially viable.

Keep a contingency Plan – Keep in mind the risk factors and chances of professional difficulty; always keep a flexible and a sensible back-up plan handy.

A Cohesive Team- There is no denial to the fact that a reliable and a well-knit team is an asset. It helps in executing a project successfully and in closing it properly.

ATTRIBUTES OF PROJECT MANAGEMENT

- Project Management may pertain to the proper way of handling a project of any size, small or big.

- Project Management is not a continuous process. It has a definite beginning as well as an end.

- Project Management employs several tools to measure accomplishments and monitoring of project tasks. The involved tools depend on the nature and genus of a project.

- Project Management reduces risk factors and increases the scope of success in a comprehensive style.

If you are new to project management and require an expert to help in pulling you out of the mess, you are at the right place because we are going to cover all the basics of the Project Management process. If you are clear with the fundamentals, managing complex projects will not be a daunting task for you. Now since you have an idea about the features of project management, let us discuss the sequential activities involved in the Project Management process.

CLASSIFYING ACTIVITIES OF PROJECT MANAGEMENT

Project Management activities can be further classified into following groups:
- ✓ Initiating
- ✓ Planning
- ✓ Organizing

✓ Executing
✓ Monitoring and controlling
✓ Motivating
✓ Closing

The goal of project management is to devise various procedures for the different areas. This would help in streamlined execution of project towards better accomplishment of objectives or goals.

LIMITATIONS OF PROJECT MANAGEMENT

Project Management is all about working towards the pertinent goals while respecting the various constraints imposed upon a project. Constraints may be self-imposed or naturally occurring. The primary limitations are:

▪ Extent – Extent is the word that will set the planned deliverables and also the mode to achieve them.

- <u>Time Frame</u> - Set or proposed time to reach different milestones in the project including completion.

- <u>Budget</u> - Finances and other resources like men, raw material, and equipment.

- <u>Quality</u> – The desired quality of job asked for.

- <u>Resources</u> - Procure and allocate resources at various points in orderly fashion keeping in mind the budget and smooth running of a project.

CHAPTER 2: MANAGING PROJECT DESPITE CONSTRAINTS

As stated in the previous chapter, Project is governed by constraints. Constraints are present in every practical system. A project that tries to achieve some goals will also have certain limitations. Project Management is about dealing with these restrictions. Constraints should not be a road block in the path of effective decision making for a successful project execution, completion, and management.

Iron Triangle

To get the visualization of challenges and difficulties arising while executing a project a visualization aid called iron triangle is used, also known as the Project Management Triangle. It is used to access the constraints in advance before a project is implemented for better decision making at the time of execution.

Iron Triangle or a Project Management Triangle deals with three primary constraints involved in a project. Though depending over the size of the project there may be other interdependent constraints also.

The three primary interdependent constraints shown in triangle are:

- ❖ Time involved
- ❖ Cost involved, and
- ❖ Scope of project

The center of the triangle lays quality that is the primary goal of a project activity. The entire structure can be improved a step further if quality is not considered a goal but constraint. It will be added as another dimension (or side) but the triangle will then become a pyramid.

The basic principle behind the triangle model says that as constraints are interdependent, changing one will affect the other two. Like in a triangle if you change the length of one side, it will affect the whole triangle including the other two sides.

Let's discuss each of the constraints in detail:

Time Factor: Amount of time allocated to a complete the project can be split for each task for better monitoring and control. The time taken will depend on factors like number of resources involved, experience or exposure to the work-skill set of individual, etc. It is not fully controlled factor and very crucial. Tight time constraint usually means increased cost and reduced scope.

Cost Factor: It is always important for the management team to take cost consideration before every planned step involved in a project. Budget and cost allocation will drive the number of resources allocated to a work and will have the adverse effect on the time lines and scope. A tight or stringent cost allocation could diminish number of resources involved, drag time lines and reduce scope.

Scope Factor: It defines the list of deliverables of the project and also the path to achieving this. Change in any point of scope will affect others. Generally increased scope means increase in time allocation and cost of the project.

"Pick Any Two" Euler Diagram

We can visualize the complexity that is present in a project with the help of the above discussed 'Iron Triangle'. There are unlimited possibilities in the plane bounded by any three constraints. To consider these possibilities we have to consider a better form of project triangle. It is called "pick any two". It is an Euler diagram where three sides of the triangle are denoted with three circular structures.

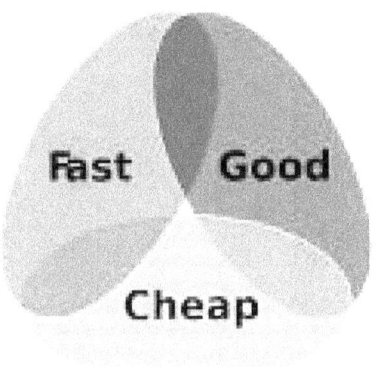

The three circular structures represent Fast, Good and Cheap, and they intersect each other at points to represent a triangle. **Fast** refers delivery time or schedule, **Good** defines quality, and **Cheap** represents the cost of designing and building a product.

This diagram connotes the ideology that 'no matter what, it is never possible to optimize all constraints. One will always lag'.

The cost cannot be minimized if a high quality product is to be delivered within a short span of time. Product will not be of high quality if time is reduced along with cost. To deliver high quality products at a cheaper price tend to take lot of time.

CHAPTER 3 – DEVISE A SIMPLE&PRACTICAL PLAN

Planning is very important before starting up with any project. It helps us to carry out the tasks involved in the project in an organized manner, ruling out the unnecessary confusion that we might confront during the course of the project.

Before we come to the steps of planning, it is imperative for us to know what might be the probable constraints if we don't have an adequate plan for the execution of our project.

Failure to meet the project deadline:
Due to lack of planning, it might not be
possible for us to complete the project
within the stipulated time. This would
have consequent and cascading effect on
other aspects of project.

Dilemma: You might land up in a mess.
Instead of smooth execution, your project
might be the reason for your sleepless
nights. So, think ahead but do not
anticipate senselessly.

Equation with client: If your client is
unhappy with the way you work, it might
affect the relationship you share in the
long run.

Derogatory performance: Your
performance will go down. Thus, affecting
your performance, incentive or
promotion.

Adverse effect on business: Business is
likely to be affected adversely if projects
are not executed in a systematic way. The
lack of planning and management will
take the toll on the business and its
associated activities.

With the right planning, any challenge in project management can be dealt with accordingly.

AN EFFECTIVE MANAGEMENT PLAN

The steps to design a simple, practical and easy to follow plan are discussed below:

- ❖ **Setting of a goal**: If you know what exactly you want to accomplish and you can portray the same to your team members, almost 60 percent of the work is done. The concept should be well-defined and vivid to your team members as well.

- ❖ **Allocation of Manpower Resources**: Determination of right number of manpower according to the work requirement is mandatory for a successful project execution. After deciding on the number of needed manpower resources, assigning each one of them their part of the job is equally important. Work distribution if done in a proper way can do wonders.

❖ **Requirement list**: Talk to each of your personnel for their specific needs and requirements to accomplish the assigned tasks. Accordingly, prepare a requirement list so that you are fully equipped right from the beginning of the project.

❖ **An Effective Action plan:** Depending on the time frame, your action plan should be clear so as to accomplish the tasks sequentially. You should be able to visualize the entire path leading to the completion of the project.

❖ **Recognizing of risk factors**: You should be aware of the probable risk areas, assess them and take necessary measures to keep the risks minimized.

❖ **Communicating with stakeholders**: Everyone should be aware of the objectives, benefits and their individual involvement in the project.

❖ **A Backup system**: A backup system should be created before beginning with a project as a preventive measure from losing any important data in case of professional crises or jeopardy. In this way, not only your data will remain secure but will also ensure an uninterrupted execution of a project during the emergency.

CHAPTER 4: HONOUR THE DEADLINES

Deadlines can be frustrating at times especially when the work load is more as compared to the time frame assigned for its completion. In spite of tight deadlines, delivering quality work is crucial for a successful project.

Listed below are simple ways to meet the deadlines ensuring that the work is done.

Start with a Plan: Planning is the key to meet project deadlines. Even though, planning might cost you some time, it worth spending every minute. Stay aware of the steps that would lead to your final destination. Do all the brainstorming required to accomplish the task sequentially. The approach should be clear right from the beginning. It is advisable that you pen-down to-do list for clarity of thoughts.

Gauge time: Suppose the actual project deadline is in the sixth month. The estimated deadline should be in the fifth month itself. You should be done with all pertaining processes so that you can utilize the remaining time in revising and reviewing all the data. To estimate the total time for project completion, it is necessary to estimate the time frame each task will take. Each team member should be clear with the time management concept.

Monitor the progress: Internal deadlines also referred as milestones, for the completion of each task by every team member help in monitoring the progress of the project. Interaction on a daily basis with the stakeholders makes you aware of the issues they are facing and helps in keeping a track of work progress. This also helps you in solving the issues as they pop up and sometimes even before they strike.

Management of Manpower Resources: The team members should never feel the lack of necessary documents accomplish the assigned task. Proper communication in terms of passing on the right amount of knowledge and sharing required documents with all your team mates will help them manage their work efficiently.

Handling problems: Sometimes things don't fall in place irrespective of all the prior planning. This kind of situation might happen anytime. The wisest thing for you to do is- know what the problem is, assess its cause and come up with possible solutions. The sooner it is done, the better it is for meeting the project deadline.

Will power and determination: A focused leader with his focus and determination will inspire the team. Inspiration can be miraculous. If the leader keeps inspiring the team, they are likely to maintain their focus and work dedicatedly to meet the project deadline.

Optimism: Positive attitude is an important characteristic of each individual. It gives you an edge over a lost game. In the end, attitude matters. As a beginner, you might require some time to inculcate optimism within you but it surely comes along with practice. If you are a leader and handling a bunch of people, positive attitude is a must. If you believe that the work can be done on time, your attitude will make your team believe too.

CHAPTER 5: MANAGINGABRUPT HINDRANCES

Before discussing further, let us ponder over the problems and hindrances that may hinder the success of a project, let us first know about all the qualities that you need to develop in you to manage your project productively. Apart from all the techniques, tools and methodologies, it is important to develop a positive mind-set that would steer you ahead confidently.

BE A GOOD PROJECT MANAGER

Be Perceptive - Develop a sense of foresight so that any impending problem would get felt by you well before time. Having a sense of anticipation and can save you from the multiple jeopardizing situations.

Be a Schemer- Be an inherent organizer and do not leave anything to doubt. Being a smart planner and organizer will place you in a star league, and you would be able to manifest your planning in an impressive way. Being an organizer will also help you in prioritizing your tasks, thus leaving nothing unfinished.

Be a Director - Since a project may involve many dimensions and aspects, you as its manager have to be a leader. You may have to interact with teams, vendors, clients, sponsors, etc. and influence them. This can be effectively done by being a natural and an effortless leader. Your leading stance will act as an innate motivation for your team members.

Be a Conversationalist – Communication would be your key to successfully handle your project. Make ample use of your communication skills and other aids like meetings, e-mails, video conferencing, etc. to resolve the issues and to meet targets optimally. Saying and conveying what you want to convey would be a great bliss as that would lead to the culmination of your ideas and plans. Sometime effective communication saves a lot of hassles on the course of the project.

Be Realistic – It is good to be a perfectionist but only to a certain extent. Develop a logical approach towards your project so that it can be accomplished realistically. A realistic approach will keep your targets and objectives well within reach.

Be Thoughtful– Being considerate and empathetic will enable you to understand others' point of view, consequently understanding the scenario and deal with it effectively.

TAKE ON VARIED HINDRANCES

Problems can happen any time in the duration of a project. In fact, while handling a project, unexpected problems and questions almost always come along the way. Therefore, you should be ready and equipped to deal with such issues else they can potentially affect the progress of your project and finally the outcome as well. If you don't want to see your project at stake, expecting the unexpected is the wisest way out.

The stage might be wonderfully set, and you may be well-versed with the project analysis but never overlook the factor of uncertainty. Your action plans might give rise to unexpected problems that you must remain prepared to handle and resolve.

Handling unexpected problems require patience and perseverance. Identify the root cause of the problem and resolve them. Issues can be resolved while being quick and effective without affecting the project progress much. Project risk management and issue management almost resemble with only slight variation.

INVOLVED ISSUES AND RISKS

The exact nature of both issues and risks remain largely unknown. We tend to have a general idea about risks in advance and keep a partial or a complete back-up plan. On the other hand, issues are less predictable, they may arise without any prior warning. For an instance, unable to find the apt human resource for a specific task is an identifiable risk. However, when one of your human resources falls sick for a couple of weeks, it becomes an issue.

Estimation and identification of risks prior to working on the project is extremely important. It can help you with prioritizing the risk areas and create an action plan to combat them proactively. However, issues can't be estimated in advance. Therefore, they require instant resolution as and when they arise. Issue management is a planned process that helps us to deal with any unexpected problem arising during the course of the project at its earliest.

We will discuss the issue management process in detail for a clear picture:

Issues should be logged or recorded as and when they happen. They should be reported and communicated at a level where you are answerable to. This can help you with some beneficial inputs on dealing with the unexpected problem and resolving it quickly and effectively. It also ensures that issues are thoroughly investigated to avoid unnecessary trouble in future. Having a laid-back attitude towards issues can worsen the situation, and it might be too late to troubleshoot them.

Before logging an issue, you should be aware of the content in an issue log. You may include the following in your issue log:

Type of issue – There are several categories of issues that you are likely to encounter. Defining an issue in a particular category is important for assigning the right person to resolve them. The possible categories are:

- ❖ Technical
- ❖ Resource
- ❖ Change in business strategies
- ❖ Change in management
- ❖ Third party

- ✦ The name of the person who discovered the issue should be recorded. This would help in getting the first version of the snag, or the issue encountered.
- ✦ The timing of identifying the issue should be logged as well to gauge its enormity.

- Details of what happened and the potential impact should be an integral part of issue log for better understanding and effective resolving.
- Priority rating should be assigned to the issue for future reference and project learning. An issue can either be a high priority, medium priority or low priority depending on its impact on project progress and success.
- The person responsible for resolving the issue should be determined on the basis of the issue type.
- A deadline should be set for resolving the issue depending on the priority level.
- The progress of the issue resolution can be found out by tracking it on a timely basis. Thus, defining an overall status to the issue is the smartest way to figure out the current scenario. Status can either be open, investigating, implementing, escalated or resolved. This gives a clear understanding about the amount

of attention and time required to resolve the issue.

+ The resolution of the issue if already done should be recorded in a chronological order.

+ A summary of all the actions taken to address the issue can be recorded in this space.

The issue logs can be of great help in terms of emergency. If the similar issue persists someday, it can be dealt with in an orderly manner without investing much time in investigating the causes and finding the right people for resolution of the issue. The specific areas of strength of every individual can be determined from the issue log.

Once issue log is done, supplementing an issue management framework is the next thing to do. The framework depicts the actual process for dealing with the issue. It gives a clear understanding to the project team regarding the responsibilities to be performed. The Framework also provides a structure that helps in quick and effective decision-making when issues arise.

Both issue logs and issue management framework capture lessons that can be referred for future projects. They made you fully equipped and prepared for any subsequent issues or problems somewhat related to the previously logged issues. Even if the future problems are not connected to the logged issues, they ensure a practical knowledge that can undoubtedly be of great help in resolving issues that you might come along on your next project.

CHAPTER 6: FINALITY OF THE PROJECT AND OVERALL EVALUATION

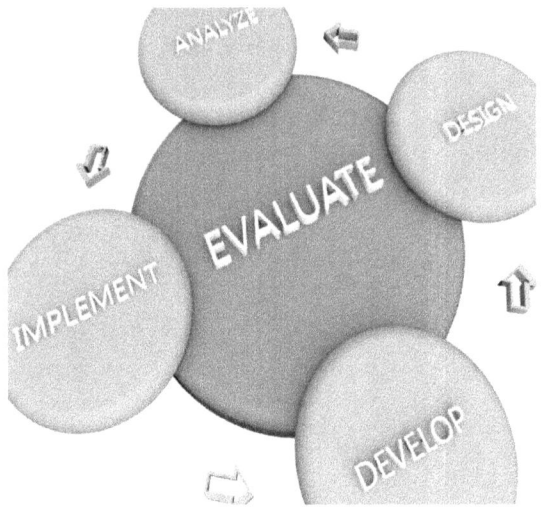

Even after all the hard work and efforts that you have been through, if the result is not properly delivered, it can still lead to client dissatisfaction which is certainly not desirable. To maintain a long-term business relationship with a client, you must ensure that the project is properly handled and the end result is fruitful as well. Consider the points listed below that you should not overlook when you are on the verge of completing your project.

EVALUATION

It is the time when you should gather your team for a comprehensive assessment of your project. Assessment is necessary to determine whether your project has fulfilled its aims and objectives or not.

Evaluation can also provide a fuller picture to the stakeholders who have rendered either financial or technical support to the project. It also acts as food for thought for the leading organization to assess the way it has implemented the project and the areas it has gone wrong so that it can design better project in future. If there are areas for quick improvement and is the need of the hour, team members can work on those areas for a successful completion of the project. The evaluation also helps in determining if the project has been able to meet the target deadline.

The methods that can be used to evaluate a project are discussed further:

Reviewing project activities – The sequential completion of each task involved in the project can be reviewed for one last time to ensure everything was done properly and nothing went wrong anywhere. A conclusion can be drawn if the team members were successful in completing the project on time, and the allocated budget was sufficient to meet all the requirements of the project. If there were issues or hurdles that came along the way of project completion, how as a team they were dealt with proactively and how they impacted the project at large.

Interviewing team members – This involves talking to each team member involved in the project. It helps to assess their level of satisfaction; the hardships they overcame for a successful completion of project; the impact of the project in their life; and their ideas to wind up the project in a better way. They should have enough ideas to develop the project further or design new projects in future. This can strengthen the relationship between you and your team members. You can record and present these interviews to your client for demonstrating your success. This can be a unique way to end your project with a practical and personalized touch.

Surveying with questionnaires – If you wish to keep a track record of the entire project related events and activities; you can ask each team member to fill up the questionnaires. On the basis of the data generated, graphs and charts can be prepared for an easy understanding of the project completion. Such dataset can also be used for preparing the final project report.

REPORTING

It includes detailed information that present a clear overview of all the aspects of the project. Reports are mainly prepared for clients so that they can understand how the project shaped up and how exactly the targets were achieved. Reports are also presented in front of stakeholders to keep up with the transparency in business. Proper reporting is indispensable for easy understanding. There are certain attributes that a good report should possess:

Clarity – The first desirable quality in a report is clarity. It should not be complicated because your purpose is to reach out to your prospect in terms of comprehensive aspects of the project. It is best to keep it short, crisp and simple. Although it is difficult, to summarize, the entire development of the project, you should be wise enough to choose your information. Your goal should be presenting how exactly you completed the project successfully.

Structure – Reports must have a clear structure for depicting the right amount of information. They should include project code, timeframe, members involved in the project, targets set for the specific timeframe and the way the targets were achieved.

Lessons learned – A good report comprises of a section that is dedicated to a critical assessment of the project as a whole. It states what the organization has learned during the course of project execution and communicates to the clients in what ways the organization can shape further projects on the basis of the lessons learned.

Besides the factors stated above, acknowledging all the efforts and hard work of your team members must never be missed out. Successful completion of the project is nearly impossible without a team. When the entire team joins hands in working on a particular project, it progressively reaches its end. Therefore, in the end, it is your team that is the backbone for your project's success, and you must give its due credit.

MORE PROJECT MANAGEMENT TIPS

- ✓ Set up your realm and do not get swayed by pre-defined criteria of successful project management. Know your priorities and set milestones. Otherwise, your project might experience difficulties that can lead to frustration, ineffectiveness and stress.
- ✓ Attain a flexible approach for better functionality. A rigid approach as a project manager may not render realistic results.
- ✓ When you set up the project criterion in the initial stage, they should be realistic and well-documented. Do not keep any intangible criterion to avoid trouble at work.

✓ , Do not commit what you can't accomplish. In a nutshell, be realistic and vouch for only achievable results.

✓ Separate situations and people from the problems. Develop newer and out-of-box options that bring in gains for the project.

✓ In case when different project realities undergo some changes, plan for renegotiating your commitments.

✓ Do not limit your managerial skills to just scheduling of your project or in breaking down the structure of project tasks. Give your consideration to other vital factors like - Staff, resource estimates, assumptions, target dates, project metrics, and relationship with vendors and subcontractors.

✓ If you are managing multiple projects at the same time, adopt a dedicated plan template for each project.

✓ Do not overburden your project with irrelevant documentation.

✓ Instead of setting massive milestones, set up small

milestones that is fair and just for your project. Your estimation and managing will be more effective on breaking larger tasks into multiple smaller ones.

✓ Do not ignore or sideline quality control. The common mistake that is often committed to project management is the pushing of quality control to the last, just before the closing of the project, especially in case of deliverable projects. This throws the rework schedule off-balance.

✓ Deal with challenges in a proper manner. Mere identification of the impending risk won't be enough. It is important to keep a vigilant eye on the relative perils and threats that might come your way.

✓ The initial money and time spent to start the project may not show instant results. There will be indeed some short-term loss in the productivity. However, benefits will start showing gradually.

✓ Base your project estimate on the effective time that would include

any emergency situation or
unforeseen interruptions.